Book Two

The Chester Books of

CELEBRATED SONGS

Selected and edited by
SHIRLEY LEAH

CONTENTS

CHESTER MUSIC

PREFACE

The Chester Books of Celebrated Songs are a graded series of volumes designed to provide a growing repertoire of fine songs in a progression related to their musical and technical difficulty and their suitability for the student singer. The books include music from the sixteenth to the twentieth centuries along with some folk song arrangements, most of which may be sung by either male or female voice. French, German, Italian and Spanish texts underlay the vocal line as appropriate, and English translations are provided, where necessary, as a guide to the content of the songs rather than as alternative performing versions.

Brief notes indicate the principal technical and interpretative features of each song for the guidance of teachers and pupils using the collections as part of a progressive vocal course. The difficulty of the piano accompaniments has also been borne in mind when selecting material for these volumes, and most of the chosen songs have only moderately difficult piano parts, so that they may easily be tackled by singers working with pianists of limited experience and by teachers who act as their own accompanists.

Although primarily designed for the young singer, these books should appeal to all singers who do not already possess the individual songs, for above all, the aim has been to present a well balanced collection of some of the most beautiful vocal music of the last four hundred years which will be enjoyed by performers and audiences alike.

Cover picture: Wheatfield with lark *by Vincent van Gogh — by kind permission of the National Vincent van Gogh Museum, Amsterdam.*

CHOPCHERRY

Peter Warlock

English   range

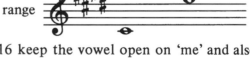

Fast and light — but not so fast that your pianist cannot keep up with you. Watch out for the syncopation in bars 5 & 8. In the final phrase, do not breathe during the semiquaver rests.

COME AWAY, COME SWEET LOVE

John Dowland

English   range

Enjoy these lovely words and keep the song simple and fresh. Note the change of beat at bar 7.

DEATH AND THE LADY

Anon

English   range

A tricky entry! Keep it moving in a free style. Beware of the octave leap followed by the diminished seventh arpeggio.

VERDI PRATI

George Frederick Handel

Italian   range

Keep the song moving, as it will easily drag. In bar 16 keep the vowel open on 'me' and also in bar 19 on 'la'.

THE PRINCESS

Edward Grieg

English   range

The setting of the same poem that Delius used in *Twilight Fancies*. It has a haunting tune — do not rush the appoggiatura, it belongs to the melody.

JAGDLIED

Felix Mendelssohn

German   range

A gay strophic song with a slightly different opening phrase for the third verse. Note the horn call which was popular at this period with many German composers. After the pauses in the last verse, pick up the tempo immediately and do not slow down on the last phrase, or the effect will be spoilt.

OH FAIR ENOUGH ARE SKY AND PLAIN
E. J. Moeran

English   range

Aim at creating a dreamy, contemplative atmosphere. There are some tricky key changes and very little help from the piano.

VIENI, VIENI
Antonio Vivaldi

Italian   range

Be careful not to accent each beat. Breathe before the 'E' in bar 10, and in bar 11, note the G♮ on the first beat, and G♯ on the second.

DER MUSIKANT
Hugo Wolf

German   range

A good exercise in legato singing over wider intervals. Take care not to slow down in the last bar of each verse, and listen carefully to the key changes in bars 18 - 20 and 40 - 44.

LYDIA
Gabriel Fauré

French   range

A charming and graceful song with words by Leconte de Lisle. The melody is based on an ascending scale. Keep the triplets even and the whole song *piano*, with only a slight crescendo on *mon âme en baisers m'est ravie.*

AN DIE MUSIK
Franz Schubert

German   range

This lovely *lied* with words by Schober requires a firm, warm tone — 'in praise of music'. Note the echo of the vocal line in the left hand accompaniment.

IMMORTAL GODS
Mario Castelnuovo-Tedesco

English   range

A strong, declamatory style is required in this song. Note the enharmonic change in bars 13 - 15. Crescendo *down* the scale on *Amen* and *up* to fortissimo in the last phrase!

CHOPCHERRY

Words by
GEORGE PEELE (1595)

PETER WARLOCK
(1894-1930)

then my true love said,_____ Till that time come a-gain She

could not live a maid._____ Then, o then, o

then my true love said,_____ Till that time come a-gain She

could not live a maid._____

COME AWAY, COME SWEET LOVE

**From THE FIRST BOOK OF
SONGS OR AYRES (1613)**

JOHN DOWLAND
(1563-1626)
tr. Carl Shavitz.

Come a - way, come sweet love, the gold - en morn - ing breakes.
All the earth, all the ayre, of love and plea - sure speakes.

Teach thine armes then to em - brace, and sweet___ ro -
Eyes were made for beau - ties grace, View - ing___ ru -

sie lips to kisse, and mix our___ soules in mu - tuall blisse.
ing loves long pains, pro - cur'd by___ beau - ties rude dis - daine.

The bass line may be doubled by a viola da gamba or cello

Come away, come sweet love,
The golden morning breakes.
All the earth, all the ayre,
Of love and pleasure speakes.
Teach thine armes then to embrace,
And sweet rosie lips to kisse,
And mix our soules in mutuall blisse.
Eyes were made for beauties grace,
Viewing ruing loves long pains,
Procur'd by beauties rude disdaine.

Come away, come sweet love,
The golden morning wastes,
While the Sunne from his sphere,
His fiery arrowes casts:
Making all the shadowes flie,
Playing, staying in the grove,
To entertaine the stealth of love.
Thither sweet love let us hie,
Flying, dying in desire,
Wingd with sweet hopes and heav'nly fire.

Come away, come sweet love,
Doe not in vaine adorne
Beauties grace that should rise,
Like to the naked morne:
Lillies on the rivers side,
And faire Cyprian flowres new blowne,
Desire no beauties but their owne.
Ornament is nurse of pride,
Pleasure measure loves delight:
Haste then sweet love our wished flight.

John Dowland
The First Booke of Songs of Ayres 1613

DEATH AND THE LADY

OLD ENGLISH FOLK SONG
arr. Michael Holloway

12

old_____ man by the way.

mp

cresc._ _ _ _ _ _ _ _ _

15

f slightly faster

My name is Death__ cannot you see

Lords, dukes and

f

18

la - dies bow down to me,

and you are

one__ of those bran - ches

21

Tempo I

three

And you fair_ maid, and you fair_ maid, and you fair

maid____ must come with me. Fair la-dy

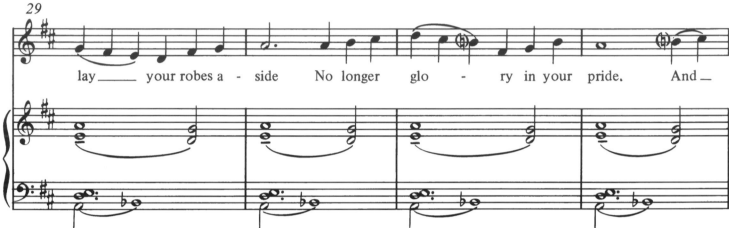

lay____ your robes a - side No longer glo - ry in your pride. And____

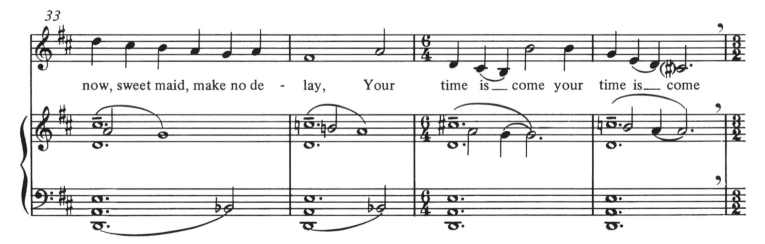

now, sweet maid, make no de - lay, Your time is __ come your time is __ come

Your time is come and you must__ a - way.

VERDI PRATI

GEORGE FREDERICK HANDEL
(1685-1759)

Verdi prati, selve amene,
Perderete la beltà;
Vaghi fior, correnti rivi,
La vaghezza, la bellezza,
Presto in voi, si cangerà.

E cangiato il vago oggetto,
All'orror del primo aspetto,
Tutto in voi ritornera.

Verdant meadows, pleasant forests,
Must soon lose your beauty;
Lovely flowers, fast flowing rivers,
Your beauty, your fairness,
Will soon be changed.

Changed though this beauty is,
Causing grief at first glance,
All will yet return again.

Ver - di pra - ti, sel - ve a - me - ne, Per - de -

- re - te la ___ bel - tà! Va - ghi fior, cor - ren - ti

ri - vi, La va - ghez - za, la bel - lez - za,

Presto in vo - i si ___ can - ge - rà. Ver - di

pra - ti, sel - ve a - me - ne, Per - de - re - te

la __ bel - tà. E can - gia - to il vago og - get - to,

poco cresc.

All' or - ror del pri - mo a - spet - to, Tut - to in voi ri -

tor - ne - rà, Tutto in voi ri - tor - ne - rà.

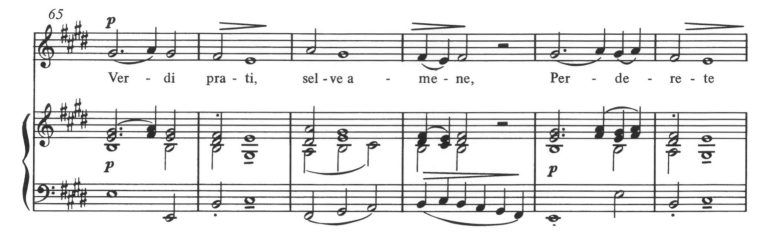

Ver - di pra - ti, sel - ve a - me - ne, Per - de - re - te

la bel - tà Per - de - re - te la bel - tà!

THE PRINCESS

English Words by
E.M. SMYTH

EDWARD GRIEG
(1843-1907)

Used by kind permission of Peters Edition, London, Frankfurt and New York.

prin - cess is sit - ting a - lone in her bower. The val - ley is si - lent and

hush'd___ is the lay. "Play on! for thy mu - sic gave

wings to the thoughts, that fain would be wan - d'ring far,___ far a-way, as the sun goes

down, as the sun goes down."___ The

prin - cess is sit - ting a - lone in her bower. Once more in the val - ley re -

e - choes the lay. Then bit - ter - ly wept she and

sighed_ in the night. "My heart, why so hea - vy? Ah! well_ well - a - day!" And the

sun went down, and the sun went down._

JAGDLIED

FELIX MENDELSSOHN
(1809-1847)

Mit Lust thät ich ausreiten durch einen grünen Wald,
darin da hört ich singen drei Vög'lein wohlgestalt.
Und sind es nicht drei Vögelein, so sind's drei Fräulein fein,
soll mir die Ein' nicht werden, so gilt's das Leben mein.

Die Abend-strahlen breiten das Goldnetz über'n Wald,
und ihm entgegen streiten die Vöglein, dass es schallt.
Ich stehe auf der Lauer, ich harr'' auf dunkle Nacht,
Es hat der Abendschauer, ihr Herz wohl weich gemacht?

In's Jubelhorn ich stosse, das Firmament wind klar,
Ich steige von dem Rosse, und Zähl die Vögel schaar.
Die Ein' ist schwarzbraun Anne, die Andre Bärbelein,
Die Dritt' hat keinen Namen, die soll mein eigen sein.

Riding gaily through a green forest,
I hear three birds singing.
And if they are not birds, they must be three maidens,
If one of them will not have me, then sad my life will be.

The sunset rays spread golden nets over the forest,
The birds sing loudly to greet them.
I stay on watch, and listen as night falls,
The twilight will have softened her heart?

I play my bugle as daylight comes,
Climb off my horse and count the birds.
One is dark-brown Anne, the other Barbara.
The third one has no name, and she shall be mine.

sin - - - gen drei Vög' - lein wohl - ge - stalt.
strei - - - ten die Vög - lein, dass__ es schallt.

Und sind es nicht drei Vö - ge - lein, so
Ich ste - he auf der Lau - er, ich

sind's drei Fräu - lein fein, soll mir die Ein' nicht wer - -
harr' auf dunk - le Nacht, es hat der A - bend - schau - -

- den, so gilt's das Le - ben mein,__
- er ihr Herz wohl weich ge - macht,__

so gilt's das Le - - - ben mein.
ihr Herz wohl weich __ ge - macht.

18

3. In's Ju - bel-horn ich

sto - - sse, das Fir - ma-ment wird klar, _____

ich stei - ge von dem Ros - - se, und zähl' die Vö - gel-

schaar. _____ Die Ein' ist schwarzbraun' An - ne, die

And - re Bär - be - lein, die Dritt' hat kei - nen Na - - men,

die soll mein ei - gen sein,_____ mein ei - gen

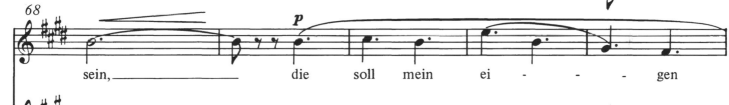

sein,_____ die soll mein ei - - gen

sein.

OH FAIR ENOUGH ARE SKY AND PLAIN

Words by
A.E. HOUSMAN

E.J. MOERAN
(1894-1950)

The__ pools and riv - ers wash so clean The

trees and clouds and air,_____ The like on earth was

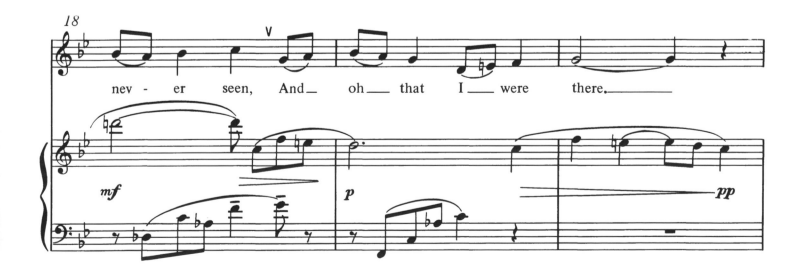

nev - er seen, And__ oh__ that I __ were there._____

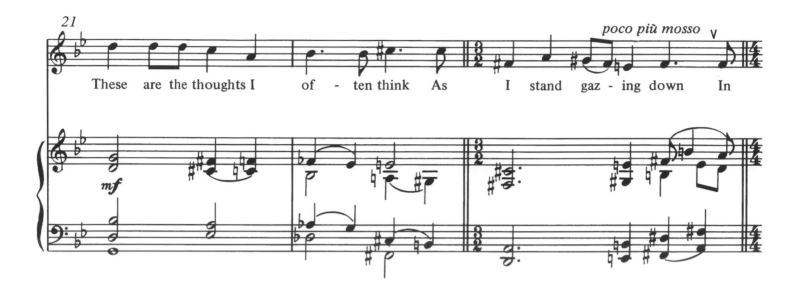

These are the thoughts I of - ten think As I stand gaz - ing down In

act up - on the cres - sy brink To strip and dive and

drown;____ But _

in the gol - den sand - ed brooks And az - ure meres __ I

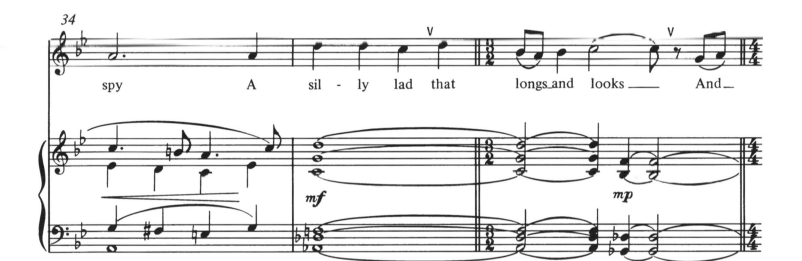

spy   A   sil - ly   lad   that   longs __ and looks ____   And __

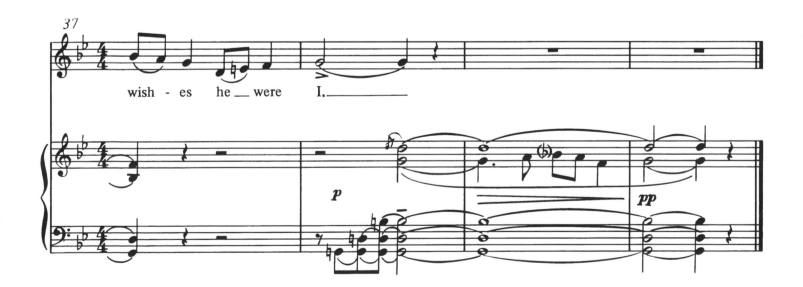

wish - es   he __ were   I. _____

VIENI, VIENI O MIO DILETTO

ANTONIO VIVALDI
(1680-1741)
arr. Michael Holloway

Vieni, vieni O mio diletto
Che il mio cor e tutto affetto,
Gia t'aspetta e ognor ti chiama.
Il mio cor e tutto affetto.

Come, come O my delight
For my heart is all affection,
It awaits you and calls to you
My heart is all affection.

Il mio co - r'e tu -tto a - ffe - tto. Il mio co - r'e tu - ttoaffe - tto

gia____ t'a - spe - tta e gia____ ti____ chia____ ma,____ ti

chia - ma.

DER MUSIKANT

Words by
EICHENDORFF

HUGO WOLF
(1860-1903)

Wandern lieb' ich für mein Leben,
lebe eben, wie ich kann, wollt'ich mir
auch Mühe geben, passt es mir doch gar nicht an.

Schöne alte Lieder weiss ich, in der Kälte, ohne Schuh'
draussen in die Saiten reiss' ich, weiss nicht,
wo ich abends ruh'!

Manche Schöne macht wohl Augen, meinet,
ich gefiel' ihr sehr, wenn ich nur was wollte taugen,
so ein armer Lump nicht wär'!

Mag dir Gott ein'n Mann bescheren, wohl mit Haus
und Hof verseh'n!
Wenn wir zwei zusammen wären,
möcht mein Singen mir vergeh'n.

I love to wander for my living,
simply living as I can, I should like
to live carefully, but it does not suit me.

Lovely old songs I know; in the cold, barefoot –
outside, I pluck the strings, not knowing
where I shall rest at night.

Many a beauty makes eyes at me, thinks
I would suit her. If I wanted to be something
I wouldn't be such a tramp!

May God send you another man, with house
and home provided.
If we two were together,
I should soon forget to sing.

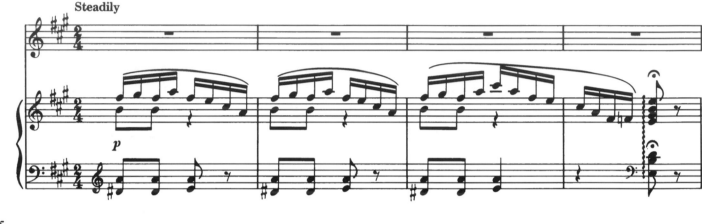

macht wohl Au - gen, mei - net, ich ge - fiel' ihr sehr, wenn ich nur was woll - te tau - gen,

so ein ar - mer Lump nicht wär'.

Mag dir Gott ein'n Mann be - sche - ren, wohl mit Haus und

Hof ver - seh'n! Wenn wir zwei zu - sam - men wä - ren, möcht' mein Sin - gen

mir ver - geh'n.

LYDIA

Words by
LECONTE DELISLE

GABRIEL FAURÉ
(1845-1924)

Lydia, sur tes roses joues	*Lydia, on your rosy cheeks*
Et sur ton col frais et si blanc	*And on your neck fresh and so white*
Roule étincelant	*Rolls sparkling*
L'or fluide que tu dénoues;	*The golden flow that you unbind;*
Le jour qui luit est le meilleur;	*The day that is dawning is the best;*
Oublions l'éternelle tombe,	*Let us forget the eternal tomb,*
Laisse tes baisers de colombe	*Let your dove-like kisses*
Chanter sur ta lèvre en fleur.	*Sing on your blossoming lips.*
Un lys caché repand sans cesse	*A hidden lily she is unceasingly,*
Une odeur divine en ton sein;	*A divine fragrance in your bosom;*
Les delices comme un essaim	*Delights in abundance*
Sortent de toi, jeune déesse.	*Flow from you, young goddess.*
Je t'aime et meurs, O mes amours.	*I love you and am dying, O my love.*
Mon âme en baisers m'est ravie!	*My soul by kisses is enraptured!*
O Lydia, rends-moi la vie,	*O Lydia, give me back my life,*
Que je puisse mourir toujours!	*That I may die over and over again!*

Le jour qui luit est le meil-leur, Ou-bli-ons l'é-ter-nel-le tom - be,

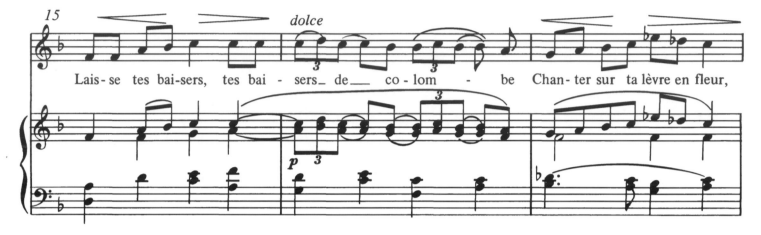

Lais-se tes bai-sers, tes bai - sers_ de_ co-lom - be Chan- ter sur ta lèvre en fleur,

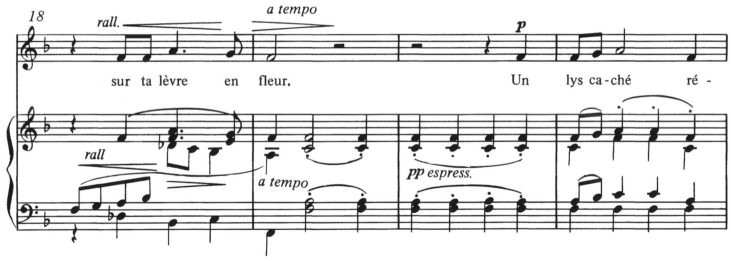

sur ta lèvre en fleur. Un lys ca-ché ré -

pand sans ces - se Une o-deur di-vine en ton sein;

Les de - li - ces comme un es-saim Sor - tent de toi, jeu - ne dé - es - se.

Je t'aime et meurs, ó mes a-mours, Mon âme en bai - sers m'est ra - vi - e!

O Ly ·di -a, rends - moi la vi - e, Que je puis - se mou-rir, mou - rir tou -

jours!

AN DIE MUSIK

Words by
F. von SCHOBER

FRANZ SCHUBERT
(1797-1828)

Du holde Kunst, in wieviel grauen Stunden,
wo mich des Lebens wilder Kreis umstrickt,
hast du mein Herz zu warmer Lieb entzunden,
hast mich in eine bessre Welt entrückt!

Oft hat ein Seufzer, deiner Harf entflossen,
ein süsser, heiliger Akkord von dir
den Himmel bessrer Zeiten mir erschlossen,
du holde Kunst, ich danke dir dafür!

O kindly Art, in how many a grey hour,
when I in life's unruly round am caught,
have you fired my heart with ardent love,
and borne me to a better world.

Often has a sigh from your harp,
a sweet, holy chord from you
a heaven of better times opened for me,
O kindly Art, for that I thank you.

20
p
Oft hat ein
fp
fp
pp
24
Seuf - - zer, dei - ner Harf ent - flos - sen, ein sü - sser.
28
hei - li - ger Ak - kord_ von_ dir den Him - mel
32
bess - - rer_ Zei - ten mir_ er - schlossen, du hol - de Kunst, ich_
cresc.
36
mf
dan - ke dir da - für, du hol - de Kunst,_ ich dan - ke dir!
p
40
fp
fp

IMMORTAL GODS

MARIO CASTELNUOVO-TEDESCO
(1895-1968)

Im - mor - tal gods, I crave no pelf;___

I pray for no man but my-self.___ Grant I may ne -ver prove so fond, To___

trust man to his oath or bond;___ Or a har - lot for her

weep - ing, Or a dog that seems a sleep - ing, Or a___

keep - er with my free - dom, Or my friends if I should need 'em.___

A - - - men! So fall to't:

Rich men sin, and I eat root.___

Printed by Caligraving Limited Thetford Norfolk England

The Chester Books of Madrigals
Edited by Anthony G. Petti

The Chester Books of Madrigals offer an exciting collection of secular European madrigals, partsongs and rounds from the 16th and early 17th centuries, newly edited from early sources by Anthony G. Petti, who contributes copious historical notes to each volume.

The majority of the settings are for SATB, and simplified keyboard reductions with suggested tempi and dynamics are provided as a rehearsal aid or as a basis for a continuo part where appropriate. Texts are in the original languages, English, French, German, Italian and Spanish, with modernised spelling and punctuation. In the case of the non-English texts translations are provided at the head of each piece.

An important feature of this anthology is the arrangement by subjects, which, it is hoped, should be of great assistance in programme planning. Indispensable popular works are interspersed with relatively unfamiliar but attractive and singable pieces.

Les Livres de Madrigaux de Chester proposent une collection très intéressante de madrigaux européens, de chansons à plusieurs voix et de canons des 16ᵉ et 17ᵉ siècles, récemment éditée par Anthony G. Petti qui s'est inspiré de sources anciennes et qui apporte d'abondantes annotations historiques à chaque volume.

La majorité sont écrits pour chœur à quatre voix mixtes et nous présentons des parties de piano pour répétition avec des suggestions de tempi et de dynamique afin d'aider la répétition ou comme base pour *continuo* si nécessaire. Les textes sont dans la langue d'origine, anglais, français, allemand, italien et espagnol, avec une orthographe et une ponctuation modernes. Pour les textes qui ne sont pas en anglais, des traductions figurent en tête de chaque morceau.

Une caractéristique importante de cette anthologie est la présentation par thèmes qui devrait faciliter l'organisation du programme. Des œuvres populaires célèbres côtoient de beaux morceaux relativement inconnus et agréables à chanter.

Die Chester Books of Madrigals bieten eine interessante Sammlung weltlicher Madrigale, Kanons und anderer mehrstimmiger Lieder aus dem 16. und frühen 17. Jahruhundert, herausgegeben anhand früher Quellen von Anthony G. Petti, der jedem Band umfassende geschichtliche Beiträge vorangestellt hat.

Der größte Teil der Chorsätze ist für SATB. Hinzugefügt wurde ein leichter Klaviersatz mit Tempovorschlägen und dynamischen Angaben für die Probenarbeit oder als Grundlage für eine Continuostimme, dort wo sie passend erscheint. Alle Texte sind in der Originalsprache wiedergegeben, englisch, französisch, deutsch, italienisch und spanisch, in zeitgemäßer Schreibweise und Zeichensetzung. Übersetzungen der nicht englischen Texte sind den jeweiligen Liedern vorangestellt.

Ein wichtiges Merkmal dieser Anthologie ist die Aufteilung nach Themen, was eine große Hilfe bei der Programmgestaltung sein sollte. Unentbehrliche bekannte Werke sind vermischt mit relativ unbekannten aber interessanten und singbaren Stücken.

Los Libros Chester de Madrigales ofrecen una interesante colección de madrigales europeos y canciones a varias voces del siglo XVI y principios del siglo XVII, recientemente recopilados de manuscritos originales por Anthony G. Petti, quien enriquece con numerosas notas históricas cada volumen.

La mayoría de las canciones son para 4 voces S.A.T.B. y las reducciones para voces y teclado se ofrecen con tiempos y dinámicas sugeridos, como base o ayuda para ser interpretados con bajo continuo.

Los textos están en los idiomas originales, inglés, francés, alemán, italiano o español, con puntuación y escritura modernas. En el caso de los textos no ingleses se facilitan las traducciones a la cabecera de cada página.

Un logro importante de esta antología es el orden por temas, que esperamos sea de gran ayuda en la planificación de programas. Las obras populares imprescindibles se intercalan con otras relativamente poco conocidas pero muy atractivas.

1. **The Animal Kingdom**
2. **Love and Marriage**
3. **Desirable Women**
4. **The Seasons**
5. **Singing and Dancing**
6. **Smoking and Drinking**
7. **Warfare**
8. **Place Names**

An index covering Books 1 - 8 is printed in Book 8

CHESTER MUSIC

Exclusive distributors: Music Sales Limited, Newmarket Road
Bury St Edmunds, Suffolk IP33 3YB